OF HUMAN BEING

OF HUMAN BEING

An A to Z of the Power and Art of Human Being

ORLA RYAN

First published 2021 by OFFC Press

Email: offcpress@gmail.com

British Library Cataloguing in Publication Data.
A catalogue record for this book is available from the National Library of Ireland and the British Library.

Print isbn: 978-1-5272-9027-3
Typesetting and cover design by Carrowmore.ie

For my family

CONTENTS

PART 3

PART 4

PART 5

PART 6

Part One

CHAPTER I

THE POWER OF APPRECIATION

"Prophets, poets and philosophers realized thousands of years ago that being satisfied with what you already have is far more important than getting more of what you want"

Yuval Noah Harari *(Sapiens)*

Being satisfied with what we already have is directly linked to how much we appreciate our everyday lives. One of the most effective ways to maintain good mental health and emotional well-being is to practice appreciation. There is no doubt that we experience higher levels of contentment when we consciously appreciate what we have. Conversely, when we take what we have for granted, the richness of our experience is greatly diminished. Given that our time here can end at any moment, it makes sense to fully appreciate the joy of existing while we still can.

Each day we get to explore this experience of living. We do this primarily through the senses. The ability to see, hear, taste, smell and touch is not a given for everyone. Each one of the senses that we are lucky enough to enjoy greatly enhances our experience of living. The best way to appreciate all that we are able to see, hear, taste, smell or touch is to be consciously present, as often as possible, in our immediate experience. Far too often, lost in thought, we operate on autopilot.

So much of the everyday things that we are lucky enough to be able to see, hear, taste, smell and touch pass by unnoticed. When this happens the depth of our own experience is lost to us. Once gone, we can never relive these particular experiences.

There are many other things that we often take for granted. Having a sanctuary to call home, food to eat, clean water to drink and freedom of speech. Around the world millions of people do not enjoy many of the things so many of us take for granted. Focused on getting more of what we want, we miss out on the value of what we already have. To lose one's sight, hearing, mobility or overall good health at any time is always a devastating loss. When this happens it can be a very painful lesson on the importance of appreciation.

So too with the loss of family and friends. Research has shown that the quality of our relationships is key in terms of overall life satisfaction. It is therefore important to bear in mind that relationships flourish when they are appreciated. Inevitably, our relationships begin to flounder when we take the people that matter in our lives for granted. Conversely, when we show our appreciation for those we care about, our relationships continue to thrive. This enhances our quality of life significantly. Good relationships not only make the good times better, they also make the bad times more bearable.

It is wise to appreciate what we have when we have it. All too often we only come to fully realise what we had when it's gone. Practising the art of appreciation makes for a life that is well lived.

THE ART OF AWARENESS

"Thinking without awareness is the main dilemma of human existence"

Eckhart Tolle

Science has proven that there is one unified field of energy in which everything exists. That energy field exists in the eternal present moment. As we are part of that energy, our creative potential depends on how much or how little we live in awareness in the present, moment by moment.

The concept of awareness and the part that energy plays in our lives is often misunderstood. Living in awareness means being consciously present, through the senses, in our immediate experience. By being consciously present, in our immediate experience, our own energy is in perfect alignment with the universal energy system. Living in awareness we are on the same wavelength as the universal energy system. In this way we are in flow with our innate creativity and our intuition which is our natural guidance system.

Our habit of incessant thinking means that for much of our lives we do not live in awareness. Becoming lost in thought is akin to changing the frequency we are on. Thinking, instead of being, means we are out of alignment with the flow of the universal energy system. In this way we lose so much of our potential creativity and intuitive guidance.

One effective way to significantly lessen the habit of incessant thinking is to practice mental silence. Mental silence can be practised at any time by simply focusing solely on the in and out breath. This allows the mind to become still and present to the flow of energy both within and around us. It may be difficult initially to prevent the mind from becoming lost in thought while practicing mental silence. When the mind drifts back into thinking, as it inevitably will, all that is required is to return one's focus to the in and out breath. Like everything else, our ability to achieve mental silence improves with practice. When our habit of incessant thinking begins to lessen we find ourselves living much more often in awareness. This means we are then more often in flow with the creative energy in the one unified field of energy in which everything exists.

To make the most of our potential we need to be consciously at one, as often as possible, with what we are being or doing at any given time. Through the senses, when we are consciously aware of what we are seeing, hearing, tasting, smelling or touching we are in perfect alignment with the energy in which our experience is unfolding.

It is important to remember that when we are stressed or anxious, worrying or ruminating on past or future events, our ability to be present in our immediate experience is greatly diminished. Worrying has no beneficial effect on outcomes. It robs us of the clarity and courage needed when we are faced with life's inevitable challenges. Prone to worry we become uncomfortable with the uncertain nature of life. We lose our natural curiosity and trust in the adventure that is life. To reawaken our original curiosity and trust in life, we need to let go of fear and accept that uncertainty is an innate part of human existence.

We experience our existence primarily through the senses. When we are not present to all that we see, hear, taste, smell and touch, our senses become dulled. We end up taking the magic that is our very existence for granted. When this happens we miss out on much of our engagement with the dance of life, this mystery that is the constant exchange and interchange of energy.

The power of awareness lies in being in flow, as often as possible, with the energy of the one unified field of energy in which everything exists. In this way our innate creativity and intuitive guidance system is always available to us throughout our lives.

CHAPTER II

THE POWER OF BELIEFS

"Beliefs are always personal but they need not be private. Shared and spread, they can change the world more than governments can"

Charles Handy

Beliefs matter as they determine so much of what we do individually and collectively. The culture of the environment we grow up in results in a belief system that is due mainly to conditioning. Our subsequent education and experience may cause those beliefs to change or to become ingrained. As fixed religious and political beliefs are often rigid, they can adversely impact on us and on society. It is vital that we begin to nurture an open and flexible attitude to what we believe.

The meaning and purpose that human existence has for us is greatly influenced by whether or not we believe that human intelligence is the highest intelligence system operating in the universe. The great thinkers, poets, and artists down through the centuries all believed in the existence of a higher energy force. Socrates, Einstein, Blake, Emerson, Mozart, C.S. Lewis and Heaney, to name but a few, all believed in the existence of a higher energy force.

It is important to recognise and acknowledge that all religious dogma is a human construct. When religion is used to connect to or express a belief in the existence of a higher intelligence it can be benign and beneficial. When however, as often happens, religious beliefs are used to discriminate against or to cause harm to others they become extremely dangerous beliefs that adversely impact the lives of many.

The one belief that can transform the affairs of our world is the belief that, as a single species, all human beings are by their very nature equal. This is the one belief and principle that would best guide us as we organize our human affairs.

All forms of discrimination whether on grounds of ethnicity, gender, race, religion or sexuality are merely prejudiced beliefs. These prejudices are the result of conditioned, limited and inflexible belief systems. Discrimination is illogical. It is small-minded thinking. The fundamental inequality between all of us and the one that matters is income inequality.

There will always be a need to improve how we conduct our human affairs. Measuring all political action against the guiding principle of equality is the best possible way. All too often greed is allowed to be the guiding principle in how our affairs are managed.

Our individual and collective beliefs matter as so much change is needed to end the suffering of millions of people around the world. Our tolerance of inequality, greed and the despair of so many shames us all.

THE ART OF BEING

"Be here now"

Ram Dass

As human beings we create and generate energy in each present moment. The importance of the kind of energy we generate cannot be overstated. That energy profoundly impacts our own lives and the lives of those around us. It also impacts the quality of the energy in the one unified field of energy in which everything exists.

We create and generate energy in each present moment through our thoughts, feelings and actions. That energy may be beneficial or it may be harmful. By consciously generating beneficial rather than harmful energy we can have a hugely positive impact on ourselves, on others and on the wider universe.

When it comes to the energy we are generating each day through our thoughts, feelings and actions, we would do well to remember that energy operates like a magnet. The kind of energy we generate is reflected in the kind of energy we draw around us. It is in our own interest to generate good energy lest we attract harmful energy by default. Just like the universe and everything in it, we too are always evolving.

We are free to create and generate energy through kind or unkind thoughts, feelings and actions. There is a world of difference between the energy generated through love and peace and the energy we generate through fear and hate. The legacy we each leave behind is all of the positive and negative energy we have created and generated throughout our lifetime. This is why it truly matters whether we operate on a daily basis from kind or unkind thought processes.

CHAPTER III

THE POWER OF CHOICE

"Every day brings new choices"

Martha Beck

The choices we make throughout our lives determine so much of our experience. Our physical, mental and emotional health is impacted positively or negatively by how we choose to think, feel and act each day. When we choose to think, feel and act from a positive frame of mind, we create a significant beneficial effect on the chemistry in our bodies that positively impacts our immune system and our overall mental health and emotional well-being. When we choose instead to focus our attention on the negative aspects of our daily lives we adversely impact our body's chemistry. This in turn affects our immune system making us more susceptible to illness and disease.

One of the most important choices we make at any given time is where to focus our attention. Depending on our own nature and how we were nurtured, we generally have a tendency to focus on either the positive or negative aspects of what happens to us in our daily lives. This largely determines our level of contentment or level of dissatisfaction.

For much of the time, the choice to focus on the positive or the negative is an unconscious choice. We tend to operate from our habitual thought patterns whose efficacy we rarely question. If, on reflection, we find we have a tendency to focus on the negative things that happen in our daily lives, we can choose to change our own programming. By consciously and consistently focusing our attention only on the positive things that occur each day we can successfully change our habitual thinking patterns over time. We would all do well to heed the words of the late Wayne Dyer when he said "allow only prosperous thoughts to live in your consciousness".

Like so much else, our mode of thinking, whether positive or negative, becomes a habit. While habits are not always easy to change, we can choose to change any habit at any time. Once we are determined to persist, it is possible to change any habit including a habitually negative outlook on life. Changing a persistently negative frame of mind to an equally persistent optimistic frame of mind is one of the most important choices that we can make.

To develop a positive outlook we can consciously begin to choose to focus on the good in ourselves, in others and in the world around us. Pessimistic thinking patterns that involve self-pity, resentment or worry do not serve us well. Conversely, developing thinking patterns that are non-judgemental and focus mainly on the good in ourselves, in others and in the world, helps to expand our horizons. We engage more in big-picture thinking when we choose to focus on the positive side of life.

Faced with life's inevitable challenges, it can often be difficult to focus on the positive. When we make the effort and succeed in doing so, it benefits us far more than when we remain focused on the negative. By choosing to focus on potential solutions rather than continuing to ruminate on our problems we feel more in control and are more empowered to deal with our issues as they arise.

The importance of the choices we make in how we think, feel and act cannot be overstated. These choices affect our own energy vibration.. Where energy is concerned like attracts like. The energy vibration that emanates from us is the kind of energy we draw back to us. Energy is a continuum that runs from the highest energy which is unconditionally loving right down to the lowest energy of fear. Often we draw low level energy to us by default when we fail to consciously choose higher energy thinking patterns.

The power of choice, which all of us have, is a useful tool that we can use to build a better life and ultimately a better world.

THE ART OF CREATIVITY

"Whatever you can do or dream, begin it. Boldness has genius, magic and power in it"

Goethe

Our creative self is always longing for expression through action. Creativity begins with a desire to do or to be something. When a persistent desire aligns well with our innate talents that is when our creative energy burns brightest. When a burning desire persists it's time to answer our innate creativity that is calling to us.

It does not necessarily mean that we can or must earn our living in this way. We may eventually do so but starting out should not involve the pressure to make money. This can be problematic as the pressure to make money often impedes creativity. The sheer pleasure of engaging with our own natural creativity is its own reward.

In his book, *Think and Grow Rich*, Napoleon Hill pointed to the most fundamental truth about creativity : "the moment one definitely commits, then Providence moves too. " He goes on to say that it is ignorance of this fact that kills countless ideas and plans.

Opportunities present themselves to us that would otherwise not come our way once we commit to achieving our desire. Whenever obstacles arise, as they inevitably will, persistence is the key to success.

Creating a clean and clutter-free environment is always a good place to start when any kind of work space is required. A cluttered space, like an overly busy mind may block the natural flow of creative energy.

One way of discovering how best to use our innate creativity is to contemplate what it is we would most regret that we did not at least attempt to achieve at some point during our lifetime. Once we decide what it is we would like to achieve, we can begin to focus our attention like a laser beam on our idea. This helps to kickstart the process as we begin to attract that specific creative energy to us. Einstein believed that our true power lies in the use we make of our imagination. Once we decide what it is we want, we need to focus our mental energy on that specific intention and imagine what the successful outcome might look like.

It is essential to fully believe in the possibility of achieving our desired outcome. We can continue to draw that creative energy to us by using the power of our imagination. This creative energy intensifies when we play out successful scenarios in our mind's eye. Our imagination is an extremely potent force that is greatly underused. As a result much of our human potential is lost to us and to the world. When we succeed in staying focused on our desires this passionate intensity continues to breathe life into them.

Trust and belief in the realisation of our desire is essential. So too, is letting go of any anxiety around outcomes as persistent doubts block the flow of creative energy. This is best achieved by engaging fully with the process itself and enjoying the challenge.

It is important to be on the lookout for serendipitous events or people that can help with the realisation of our desire. This is the energy that we ourselves have drawn to us.

Persistence in the face of obstacles is essential if we are not to become discouraged and simply give up. Belief and commitment will be rewarded so long as we persist in our endeavour.

Our creative pursuits, great and small, give our lives a wonderful sense of meaning and purpose. When we know what it is we want to achieve and focus on that, we experience the joy and richness of existence.

CHAPTER IV

THE POWER OF DESIRE

"Desire, burning desire is basic to achieving anything beyond the ordinary"

Joseph B. Wirthlin

All too often our long-held desires can lie dormant for years, sometimes even for an entire lifetime. All that unfulfilled potential eventually turning to dust or ashes, a mountain of regret left behind by successive generations. All too often we allow our aspirations to lie dormant through lack of ambition, lack of self-belief or lack of willpower.

Achieving anything beyond the ordinary begins with the power of desire. A burning desire ignites and attracts the creative energy that facilitates the achievement of any deeply held aspiration. Once we decide to pursue a burning desire our lives take on a deeper sense of meaning and purpose. When that burning desire is in sync with our innate talents, it is then that we have the best chance of success. What is required is action. Devising a step-by-step plan helps not only to outline the possibilities but also to clarify potential pitfalls.

Repeatedly visualising what a successful outcome looks like is extremely beneficial as visualisation intensifies and sustains creative energy. Affirmations are also extremely powerful in intensifying and sustaining creative energy. It is never enough to meekly hope or wish to achieve something. Weak desires produce equally weak results.

When we succeed in embedding a burning desire in unwavering belief we create a powerful energy magnet. Strong desire and absolute belief both act as magnets for the creative energy required for any specific project. When we allow our desires to weaken and our belief in them to waiver, doubts inevitably begin to assail us. These doubts block the flow of creative energy.

Visualisation and affirmations are two very powerful tools that are grossly underused. They stoke the creative energy of our burning desires and help to silence the doubts that block our creative flow. By engaging our imagination in the creative process we achieve far more with far less arduous effort.

THE ART OF DOING

"Contentment comes from doing a few things well"

Marcus Aurelius

If we have a purpose on this planet it has to do with our own evolution and that of the wider universe. What we think, feel, say and do matters as this is the energy we create and generate. In this way we contribute positively or negatively to our own evolution and ultimately to that of the wider universe.

Carl Jung may or may not have been right when he said "When I die my deeds will accompany me". Either way the good or harm that we do during our lifetime is the legacy we leave behind. Several times each day we get an opportunity to choose between doing good or doing harm. Whichever we choose affects not only our own evolution but also that of the universal energy system.

We can simplify our lives by doing fewer things and doing those things well. This allows us to have more control over our time. Hurtling along, juggling too many things with no clear plan or focus can leave us frazzled and dissatisfied. Planning how to do a few things well and focusing on those makes for a far more contented lifestyle.

Creating a balance between what we have to do and what we want to do is essential. Listing our obligations alongside the things that give us pleasure allows us to make time for both.

When it comes to the things we are obliged to do, like paid work or family commitments, it helps to remember the benefits that will accrue to ourselves or others. Focusing on the benefits lends a sense of generosity to fulfilling our obligations which in turn makes for a more pleasurable experience. We need to balance our obligations with our own needs by doing something each day that gives us pleasure. Pleasure is essential as it nurtures our being.

Looking at how we currently spend our time helps us to reflect on whether or not this serves us well. It is important that we each take full responsibility for what we do. This is how we can best maintain control over our own lives and decide what kind of legacy we want to leave behind. Developing our own philosophy and value system is enormously helpful in this regard. Without a philosophy or value system life can appear meaningless.

Whether or not our deeds accompany us when we die, doing good benefits the common good. Doing harm benefits no one, not least ourselves.

CHAPTER V

THE POWER OF EMOTION

"If thought doesn't give continuity to feeling, feeling dies very quickly"

Krishnamurti

Emotional well-being is central to a life that is well lived. It is therefore essential to understand the inextricable link between the thoughts we are thinking and how we are feeling. If we want to change how we feel we must first change our thoughts. By allowing only prosperous thoughts to live in our consciousness we create emotional well-being. Our feelings serve as a useful guide to when we need to change to a more positive frame of mind. By changing our thinking we are able to change how we are feeling.

As human beings we experience a range of emotions. What we are feeling is our mode of being at any given moment. This is the energy that we are generating and attracting back to us in each moment. Depending on our DNA, our conditioning and our experiences, we tend to have a propensity towards either an optimistic or a pessimistic mindset. An optimistic mindset has a positive effect on our overall well-being.

We can retrain our brain to change a habitually pessimistic mindset to an optimistic one by consciously and consistently changing how we think. If we choose to stay focused on what is good in our own lives, in the people around us and in the wider world, we can significantly improve our own well-being.

Sadness and grief are normal emotional responses to loss. They are not negative in any way. They simply reflect the depth of the loss that is felt. Grief is precious and needs to be honoured and worked through until in time we are able to come to accept our loss. Being busy may help as too much time spent ruminating on loss puts us at risk of slipping into a depression from which it can be difficult to extricate oneself.

Anger and hate, on the other hand, are deeply destructive emotions that damage us and can cause great harm to others in the process. Thinking angry or hateful thoughts serve no useful purpose. They generate the kind of energy that damages both ourselves and others. Anger destroys emotional well-being. Everything that we think and feel has a positive or negative impact on every cell in the body. For this reason alone it is always wise to allow our anger and our irritation to dissipate sooner rather than later.

Likewise when we engage in thoughts that involve blaming or resenting others. We risk falling into the trap that is self-pity, seeing ourselves as a victim. This too robs us of emotional well-being. When we decide instead to seek to understand or to simply forgive someone it is ourselves that we unburden. Holding on to hurt is often far more damaging than any original upset.

Sufficient and restful sleep is also an essential component of emotional well-being. When we are deprived of sufficient and restful sleep we can become irritated far too easily. As this can adversely affect our relationships with those closest to us it can be extremely damaging if we allow this to continue over a long period of time.

Being conscious of the link between what we are thinking and how we are feeling is essential if we want to take charge of our own emotional well-being. One of the most common and destructive thought/emotion links is the worry/stress link. There will almost always be something we can worry and stress about if we choose to. Our habit of worrying only serves to cloud our thinking and our judgement at a time when clarity of thought and good judgement are what is needed.

Worry induces fear and a sense of powerlessness while feeling stressed destroys our emotional well-being. Instead of worrying and feeling stressed we can decide to let go of fear and trust in the innate uncertainty that is life. If we do this we will be better able to think clearly and act judiciously. This will prove to be immensely freeing and is a more mature response to life's inevitable challenges.

THE ART OF ENJOYMENT

"There is no goal to reach. There is nothing to be attained.
Stay in this consciousness and enjoy this moment"

Bob Dylan

When we spend our time ruminating on past events or worrying about the future, we deprive ourselves of any potential enjoyment in the present moment. As we cannot change the past or control the future it is wiser to accept our past and embrace the uncertain nature of future events with a sense of openness and curiosity. We are then free to enjoy the flow of experience as it is happening in each present moment.

It is wise to have as long a list as possible of the things that we enjoy doing. The next logical step is to do more of the things we enjoy doing and less of the things we do not enjoy. While this is an obvious way in which we can make our lives more enjoyable, it is not always something we remember to do consistently.

On a practical level a three or four day working week would create a better balance in all our lives. This would prove to be an extremely effective way to combat the chronic stress levels being currently experienced by so many people. It would also create much needed employment for those who are unemployed. With advances in technology unemployment is likely to rise if nothing is done to solve this issue. A legal entitlement to a three or four day working week would benefit the common good.

When it comes to our perceived obligations it is worth prioritising them so that we can rid ourselves of unnecessary burdens. When there are things that we must do, like family or work commitments, it is better to act from a generous heart and acknowledge the potential benefits for both ourselves and others. In the right frame of mind almost anything can be enjoyed.

When we allow ourselves to become annoyed or irritated it is then that our obligations weigh heavy on us. Ensuring, as far as possible, a balance between our obligations and the things we enjoy doing makes for a more enjoyable life experience.

Being overly busy can lead to chronic stress and eventually to ill-health. Recharging our energy each day is fundamental to enjoying life. For this reason sufficient and restful sleep is fundamental to our emotional well-being. Spending time as often as possible close to nature nurtures our human spirit. The flowers, the trees, the rivers, the oceans, the mountains, the birds and the animals all connect us to a hunger and desire for peace which lies deep within us. Nature nurtures us and is one of life's most effective healing balms.

Most often it is we ourselves who destroy the potential enjoyment of our present moments. When we are angry or resentful we lessen significantly the potential enjoyment of our own lives. As adults we smile and laugh a lot less than children do. Given that suffering and adversity are part of the human condition it makes little sense adding unnecessarily to the grief and sadness that we must sometimes endure. Letting go of perceived hurts, past and present, is immensely freeing.

Knowing where we are on the introvert-extrovert spectrum is equally important. Extroverts recharge their batteries by spending time in the company of others. Introverts need time alone to recharge their energy. Conversely, too much time alone is draining for extroverts, while too much time in company is draining for introverts. An awareness of this fundamental difference is essential for both extroverts and introverts so that we can achieve a balance that better suits our authentic selves.

By slowing down and enjoying the flow of our everyday experience we honour ourselves and we honour life. It is equally important to remember that other people are not responsible for our enjoyment in life. We honour others by allowing them to be who they are.

Part Two

CHAPTER VI

THE POWER OF FEAR

"The fear of suffering is worse than suffering itself"

Paulo Coelho

If you live in a war-torn country or your life is threatened for any reason then fear is a natural human response. Fear in this instance may well be the thing that saves you as it prompts you to take action.

Fear-based thinking, on the other hand, ,when there is no immediate threat, greatly diminishes how we experience living. So much time and energy is wasted thinking anxious thoughts about past or future events. If we choose to worry we will always find something to worry about. Over a lifetime this accounts for so much wasted time and energy. Time that could have been used not only more pleasantly but also more productively. We have been conditioned to accept worrying as a normal response to life's uncertainty. In our efforts to avoid any experience that may be painful we automatically start to worry, in the misguided and vain hope that somehow worrying may help.

It is better to acknowledge and accept that painful experiences are inevitable in any life. It is also important to realise that worrying adversely affects our mental and emotional well-being. Worrying increases our stress level which adversely affects our immune system leaving us more susceptible to illness. Worry also results in low mood as it keeps us focused on the perceived problem. It is always better to focus instead on potential solutions and simply accept the things that are outside our control.

Worry is a deeply negative thought pattern. We can change any habitual thought pattern once we have the self-awareness and self-discipline to commit to that change. Catching ourselves every time we begin to worry and making a conscious decision to refuse to worry is key.

We cannot change the past or control the future. It is wiser to become comfortable with life's uncertain nature. It helps if we see life as an adventure where good and bad things happen.

Staying open to all experience allows us to venture forth in a spirit of curiosity and courage. This way of being enables us to better handle adversity as it arises, free from the burden of fear. To always seek to avoid suffering of any kind is to fail to understand the fundamental nature of the human condition.

The natural antidote to stress and anxiety is relaxation. There are many audio versions of guided relaxation that are extremely effective in reducing and releasing stress from the body and the mind. Developing a meditation or yoga practice is enormously effective in preventing the accumulation of stress or anxiety. If we are to maintain good physical, mental and emotional health it is essential to let go of fear. Rather than spending time worrying, holding on to all that fear, it is sometimes good to talk to someone who will listen or to write down our concerns. Each one can bring a sense of release and much needed clarity.

Becoming comfortable with uncertainty is immensely freeing. The best way to achieve this is to retrieve the natural curiosity that all babies are born with and which is lost to us as we develop our mundane routines. Feeling courageous trumps feeling fearful every time.

Demanding more of ourselves is no bad thing. By keeping our awareness in the present, on what it is we are doing at any given moment we can relax into the flow of our own life experience. We know how our story ends and it is the same for all of us. Choosing to live with courage rather than fear is what counts. None of us are ever likely to regret that we did not worry more and most of us will wish we had worried less or, better still, not worried at all.

THE ART OF FOCUS

"Of everything I have ever studied, where you put your focus is what makes the biggest difference in your life"

Paul McKenna

What we choose to focus on in life determines to a large extent how we experience living. Too often our attention and focus hops from one thing to another. This weakens the power of our energy. When we decide instead to focus our energy like a laser beam on whatever we are doing in the present moment, we are then in alignment with the universal energy system from where all inspiration and innate guidance flows.

It is important not to allow our focused attention to dissipate into random thinking. Focused effort in the present where we become one with what we are doing is a deeply rich and satisfying experience. We are then in flow with what Dostoyevsky called "the river of life".

With practice it is possible to bring this kind of focused attention to all our actions and encounters. Whether we are enjoying our food, having a conversation or painting a picture, focusing our attention exclusively on our being and our doing allows us to live each moment of our lives to the fullest.

Lack of focused attention makes for a less satisfying experience of living. With thoughts flitting from one thing to the next, we miss out on much of our present moment experience. We sleepwalk through so many rich experiences when we fail to focus our attention in the present moment. The present moment is all that ever exists and each moment of our lives when we are lost in thought is a present moment that has been missed. Add it all up and years of our lives go by when we are not truly present in our immediate experience. Once past these moments are gone forever.

There is another aspect to where we focus our attention that is of immense importance. Many people tend to focus on what is lacking in their lives. This is the surest way to experience a discontented life. Being alive in and of itself is a rich experience. Focusing attention on what we have, rather than on what is lacking, and fully appreciating all of it leads to a more contented life experience.

Equally important is the fact that we can achieve our goals with far less arduous effort when we focus our mental energies on what we want to achieve. This mental focus helps to create and sustain the creative energy that is necessary if we want to succeed in our endeavours great or small.

CHAPTER VII

THE POWER OF GOALS

"The greatest danger lies for most of us not in setting our aim too high and falling short but setting our aim too low and achieving our mark"

Michelangelo

Often we take the magic that is being alive for granted. Having dreams and aspirations can reawaken our passion and enthusiasm for being in the world. Having goals helps to focus our minds on what it is we would like to achieve during our lifetime.

Dreams and aspirations are more easily achieved when we commit to the process of setting specific goals for ourselves. Pursuing a goal is a step-by-step process that helps us to better explore our potential. Without specific aspirations there is a tendency to drift aimlessly through life. Worse still we can get caught up in mundane worries and anxieties.

If we can match our aspirations as closely as possible with our innate talents and acquired skills we give ourselves the best chance of success.

Pursuing any goal requires effort and commitment to the process. The key to success can be summed up in three words: persistence, persistence, persistence. Many dreams and aspirations are abandoned when a setback occurs or a difficult obstacle presents itself. This is the very time we need to enlist the power of persistence.

Over our lifetime it is eminently possible to make a significant and positive difference in our family, our community or in the wider world. Any aspiration that benefits not just ourselves but positively impacts the lives of others is an aspiration worth pursuing.

Goals energise our being and give purpose and meaning to our lives. To begin all that is required is an idea. Ideas are the inspiration that comes when we listen to our own intuitive voice. Very often the same idea comes to us again and again, all the while trying to get our attention. Sometimes we ignore these inspired ideas or we procrastinate waiting until the time is right. It is crucial to pay close attention to the ideas that persist. It is these ideas, particularly when they match our innate talents, that tend to give our life it's true meaning and purpose.

When we encounter an idea that we are longing to pursue it is essential to act. A good way to begin is to draw up a written plan that specifies our desired outcome and how we might achieve it. This is the time to aim high. The best plans include a step by step detailed process which outlines what needs to happen so that our aspirations can be realised and how obstacles might be overcome.

Having too many goals at any one time can lead to being overly busy with no downtime. A good place to start is to identify the one thing that we will most regret not attempting to achieve in our lifetime. It is a good idea to work out the specific hours each day or each week that we can commit to any goal. Developing the self-discipline that particular commitment will require is also necessary.

Most things are achievable once we are prepared to commit to the effort and time required. Keeping our focus on what a successful outcome might look like and would feel like helps to maintain motivation, passion and enthusiasm for any project. We can also practice creative visualisation by using our imagination to present the desired scenario to our subconscious mind. The subconscious is a servo-mechanism that does not distinguish between what is real and what is imagined. As a servo-mechanism the subconscious works to help create whatever is presented to it. We can use this power to draw to us opportunities that will help us to succeed. To sustain the flow of creative energy it is vital to maintain a sense of excitement and enthusiasm around specific goals.

In addition to creative visualisation we can use daily affirmations or mantras which, when used consistently, are extremely powerful. Affirmations must be phrased in the present tense and might go something like the Emile Coué's famous "Every day in every way I am better and better". Using whatever wording is appropriate for a specific goal, the most effective time to use affirmations is on waking up and on going to sleep as the subconscious is then at its most receptive.

Life satisfaction greatly increases when one is in pursuit of a specific goal. Each day we are presented with an opportunity to pursue whatever it is that we would like to achieve during our lifetime. When we consistently pursue our deepest, long held aspirations, great or small, we are ensuring that when we come to die we need not have too many regrets.

THE ART OF GRATITUDE

"A grateful mind is a great mind which eventually attracts to itself great things"

Plato

The art of gratitude is best expressed through our appreciation of all things great and small. How we experience living changes significantly when we develop a deep sense of appreciation. A thirteen year old Irish girl named Constance was so grateful following a heart operation because all she wanted was to be able to breathe on her own. How many of us ever stop to appreciate being able to breathe on our own? We can ask ourselves this same question when it comes to the extraordinary gifts that are sight, hearing, taste, smell, touch, mobility and simply having food and shelter. So many of us have so much to be grateful for.

When we operate from a sense of gratitude we change the energy of our being. One way to experience living at a higher energy level is to consciously practice gratitude through appreciation. Developing this kind of attitude helps to displace the negative energy that comes from negative thinking. Operating at a higher energy level, by practicing gratitude, we both generate higher energy and attract higher energy back to us. Einstein believed we should thank the universe hundreds of times each day. It is possible to feel a shift in one's own energy when operating from an attitude of gratitude.

At times we take our very existence for granted, failing to appreciate the magic of being. It is often our tragedies that, all too late, enable us to fully appreciate what we have lost. There is a world of difference in the life experience of those who practice gratitude through appreciation and those who do not as we change our energy vibration when we practice gratitude. A heart that is filled with gratitude and appreciation is open and receptive to the flow of the positive life force. A heart that is ungrateful is out of sync with that energy.

We are all faced with issues and challenges which test our resilience at various times in our lives. Maintaining an attitude of gratitude through appreciation allows for a more balanced and resilient approach to life's challenges.

CHAPTER VIII

THE POWER OF HABIT

"We are what we repeatedly do"

Aristotle

Habit wields enormous power in our everyday lives. Some habits serve us well while others keep us stuck in thought patterns and patterns of behaviour that undermine our potential for a contented and fulfilling life experience.

Changing how we feel or how we behave involves changing our habitual thinking patterns. If our habitual thinking tends towards the positive then maintaining that habit is hugely beneficial. If, on the other hand, we tend to focus on the negative then we are undermining our own life experience at every turn. Making a conscious effort to shift the focus of our thoughts always towards what is positive in any and all situations fundamentally changes how we experience living. A glass that is half filled is always both half full and half empty. Habitually interpreting it as half full makes all the difference.

There is no doubt that our habitual thought patterns create either positive or negative feelings in us. Likewise our feelings, positive or negative, affect how we think. Maintaining awareness of that circular link is essential. When we take charge of how we habitually think we are better able to control how we feel.

Many of our daily habits do not support our own well being. For example, habitually thinking stressful thoughts creates distress and emotional imbalance. It has been scientifically proven that persistently negative thought patterns affect the body's chemistry undermining our own immune system.

Similarly, if we are habitually eating processed rather than fresh food, the store of vitamins and minerals in our body becomes significantly depleted. While vitamins and minerals are no guarantee against serious illness, they play a vital role in every aspect of our physical, mental and emotional well-being. Apples, berries, carrots and green vegetables are full of vitamins and minerals while a good vitamin and mineral supplement helps to ensure against the depletion of essential nutrients.

An almost inevitable consequence of some of the very stressful lifestyles that pertain today is the prevalence of fatigue. One good habit that helps to counteract fatigue is drinking at least two litres of water each day. This improves alertness and energy levels. Equally being in the habit of getting early nights rather than staying up late goes a very long way to combating fatigue.

Whether one is in the habit of leading a physically active

lifestyle or a sedentary one is also important. While a proper diet ensures we do not gain more weight than is good for us, a sedentary lifestyle prevents us from losing any excess weight that we may be carrying. It is important to remember that food is converted into energy and energy that is not used each day is stored in the body as fat.

Once we become aware of any habit we would like to change, it makes sense to focus on the benefits that changing that habit will bring. It is best to only change one habit at a time because changing any habit requires real commitment and determination. With persistence we can change any unwanted habit. By changing a pessimistic outlook to a more optimistic one, focusing on the good in ourselves, in others and in the world around us improves both our mental health and our emotional well-being.

THE ART OF HAPPINESS

"For every minute you are angry you lose sixty seconds of happiness"

Ralph Waldo Emerson

Being content in each present moment is the key to lifelong happiness. Nonetheless there are other factors that are worth considering as our personal happiness and the happiness of those we care about is of enormous importance to us.

Knowing one's authentic self and being true to that authentic self is fundamental to living a happy life. Inauthenticity is a disservice to oneself as it inhibits the emergence and blossoming of the true self. Pertinent to this is the deep sense of happiness that comes when we feel comfortable in our own skin. Being true to whether one is predominantly extroverted or predominantly introverted is fundamental. For those of us who are predominantly extroverted, spending time in the company of other people is essential while too much time spent alone depletes the extrovert's energy. For those of us who are predominantly introverted, time alone is essential to replenish energy while too much time spent in the company of others is exhausting. Recognising the balance that best suits oneself and maintaining that balance makes for a much happier life experience.

The degree to which we are happy or unhappy also depends on the quality of our relationships. When we are lucky enough to have close relationships with family or friends, we tend to be significantly happier. Relationship difficulties cause unhappiness and distress. Anger, blame and resentment over perceived grievances seriously damage potentially good relationships. Assertive communication, open, honest and direct makes for healthier relationships. Knowing when to let go of relationships that are dysfunctional despite one's best efforts is equally important. In all relationships that go wrong there is generally right and wrong on both sides. While it is sometimes best to let go of the dysfunctional relationships in our lives, others are worth fighting for, letting go instead of the anger, resentment or misunderstandings that have damaged the relationship.

We alone are responsible for how we think, feel and act. Blaming others or making them responsible for our happiness or unhappiness is deeply neurotic. A heart that is at peace with itself and with the world is more open to the magic and joy of the experience of living. Being ourselves, taking full responsibility for our thoughts, feelings and actions, blaming no one, leads to an independent and happier self. Being non-judgemental, allowing others to be who they are is also immensely freeing.

A simple lifestyle creates the time and space for a happier life. Being overly busy can be extremely stressful. Doing more of the things we enjoy doing and less of the things we do not enjoy makes for a more enjoyable life experience. Often we find ourselves pleasing others rather than pleasing ourselves. With the exception of obligations that have to be met, whether work or family, pleasing oneself makes for a happier life.

When it comes to the broader issue of creating a happier society there are some basic changes that could easily be made if we demanded fundamental change in how we organise society for the benefit of the common good. A universal basic income so that everyone of us can properly choose how we can be both happy and contribute to society at the same time. By using our innate talents as artists, business people or carers, the list is endless, we can create a happier society. When it comes to the less attractive menial work we simply need to make it well paid work and there will be no shortage of willing participants. There ought to be no such thing as low paid employment particularly when it comes to less pleasurable work. Also necessary to reduce stress and increase happiness in our societies is a three to four day working week. Being required to work five days out of seven creates an obvious work/life imbalance. A long weekend allows for much needed home catch up time that includes work relaxation and pleasure time. So many people are feeling overworked and experience high levels of stress. Others suffer anxiety because they are under employed. Having the legal entitlement to work a three to four day week would lessen stress and create much needed employment. To create a happier society also means creating co-operative enterprises rather than continuing the low pay high profit business model that predominates large sections of our society. Similarly affordable co-operative housing projects each with onsite crèche facilities would go a long way towards creating a fairer and happier society.

Inevitably life will at times be challenging for all of us. When it is, we need to dig deep and rise to the challenges we are faced with. By engaging our personal strengths rather than indulging our weaknesses we develop resilience. When we are strong, independent and true to our essential self we bring a sense of deep contentment to each present moment and are better able to deal with life's inevitable challenges.

CHAPTER IX

THE POWER OF INSPIRATION

"An intelligence system greater than the human mind is at work"

Eckhart Tolle

We are each a channel through which consciousness itself operates. Our great tragedy is that we do not engage more with this greater intelligence system. The underlying consciousness is our natural guidance system. To achieve our full potential we need to begin to engage more with the intelligence system that is greater than the human mind.

At all times we are either in or out of alignment with this

greater intelligence system. When we are consciously present in each moment we are in perfect alignment with the universal intelligence system. Sadly for most of us, our habit of incessant thinking results in our being out of alignment with our innate guidance system for much of our lives. Lost in thought we are constantly blocking the natural flow of guidance and inspiration that is always available to us.

To be more present on a consistent basis it helps if we commit to a daily practice of sitting in mental silence. By taking time out once or twice each day to sit with eyes closed in perfect stillness, we can begin to sense the flow of energy in and around us. By listening to the stillness, fixing our attention on the flow of energy or on the in and out breath, the mind begins to quieten.

Over time with regular practice it becomes easier to hear the voice of inspiration. Our being present means we are in perfect alignment with the universal consciousness from where all ideas and guidance flows. When the habit of thinking incessantly is lessened, mental clutter is gradually transformed into a new kind of mental clarity. Ideas have more room to flourish.

This power that inspires us is our natural guidance system. It is always available to us throughout our lives. Being rather than thinking is the key to aligning our own energy with the energy of the universal energy system from which all inspiration flows.

THE ART OF INTENTION

"Intent is a force that exists in the world"

Carlos Castenada

The field of intention is an energy field where ideas can be sown and nurtured. When we use the field of intention we achieve far more with far less arduous effort. By focusing our attention repeatedly on an idea, we are ' intending' that idea into being. This is where and how to expand the energy that breathes life into ideas. The energy force that is intent only ever exists in the eternal present moment. To realise any idea therefore it makes sense to spend time as often as possible in the field of intention.

When it comes to ideas, our tragedy, according to Michelangelo, is not that we aim too high but that we aim too low and are in danger of reaching our mark.

Einstein believed that imagination was more important than

knowledge. By visualising an idea clearly in the mind's eye we are intending it into being. It is equally important to believe in the realisation of one's idea as doubts block the flow of creative energy. Feeling excited about an idea infuses that idea with energy. When it comes to outcomes a flexible attitude serves us best.

It is often wiser to keep one's idea to oneself at least in the early stages of gestation. Otherwise we may become discouraged or dissuaded by others. It is also important to remain alert and ready to act when serendipitous opportunities present themselves.

When we succeed in maintaining awareness in the present we are in alignment with the powerful energy of the universe where the forces of inspiration and intent reside. With a specific plan or purpose in mind, at any given time, our lives have more immediate meaning and we feel more fulfilled. By becoming the driving force in our own lives, intending our inspired ideas, we achieve greater life satisfaction.

CHAPTER X

THE POWER OF JUSTICE

"... a government based on the principles of economic, social, racial and environmental justice – that struggle continues"

Bernie Sanders

The power of justice to transform the lives of human beings is unequalled. Our tolerance of injustice is therefore all the more remarkable. Global politics through its actions and inaction prolongs injustice. There is no shortage of wealth but to our collective shame we tolerate a shocking lack of fairness in its distribution within countries and across continents.

Any political system that presides over the co-existence of beggars and billionaires is a failed system. It is time for a new kind of politics where the silent majority regain the power that is so easily entrusted to a tiny ruling class in each country.

In theory at least most people want to live in a fair and just world. So often we feel powerless in the fight against injustice. With global technology it is now more possible than ever to make our voices heard. It is time for the silent majority to begin a worldwide movement for social justice. The principle of fairness for all must be the guiding principle of all politics. The silent majority can become vocal and march across the globe for a fairer distribution of wealth and resources.

We need to name and shame and help to depose, where necessary, despotic leaders who steal the wealth of their nation, impoverishing their people in the process. They are criminals who go unchallenged in their crimes against humanity. We turn a blind eye as millions of our fellow human beings suffer lives of poverty and deprivation. Across the globe we are but one people with equal rights and responsibilities. Equal rights and justice for all ought not be allowed to depend on the whims of our political masters.

It is not naive to think that we can create a better world. All that needs to happen is that we, the silent majority, change the way we think and act.

Co-ordinated petitions and peaceful marches across the world can be effective in the demand for change. The majority, if we act together, can significantly change how the world is organised and ruled. Countries that do not enjoy freedom of speech and movement must be able to rely on the active support of those of us who enjoy these freedoms. It is hearts and minds that need to change and the tolerance of anything less than justice needs to end. By appealing to our better nature we could create and enlist a force of billions of people in the fight for a just world. What a movement for change that would be if coordinated properly.

Who would dare to deny justice if billions across the world demanded it. We just have to want it enough to stand up and be counted.

THE ART OF JUDGEMENT

"When you judge another, you do not define them, you define yourself"

Wayne Dyer

We waste so much time and energy sitting in judgement on one another. We judge each other by how we look, what we say and what we do or don't do. We judge instantly, often critically and sometimes harshly. And all to what end? This habitual rush to judgement benefits no one and harms both ourselves and others.

Breaking the habit of automatically judging others and maintaining a non-judgemental attitude rids us of so much mental clutter. It is equally freeing when we stop caring how we are judged by others. Ruminating on what others think of us is wasting time and energy that could be better spent. This self-imposed prison-like mentality where time is spent wondering and worrying about what others are thinking is needless angst. What others think of us reflects on them not on us. It is their business and there is no reason to make it ours.

When we stop judging others and stop caring about how we are judged, we can reserve the art of judgement for decision-making purposes. Creating the mental space to develop the art of judgement makes for better outcomes. We have everything to gain and nothing to lose by reserving judgement for decision-making. Our rush to judgement diminishes our potential to relate to one another in a spirit of openness, tolerance, generosity and understanding. We can free ourselves by being true to who we are and by allowing others to be who they are.

Part Three

CHAPTER XI

THE POWER OF KINDNESS

"... three things in life matter. The first is kindness. The second is kindness. The third is kindness"

Paul Murray

We can use the power of kindness to be the change we want to see in the world. By consciously operating out of kindness in all our relationships and our daily encounters we can contribute to the creation of a global culture of kindness.

Kindness builds close bonds between people. It is a powerful healing balm. All relationships thrive or falter depending on the presence or absence of kindness.

Every day each of us is presented with countless opportunities to use the power of kindness for change. Fully functioning families are built on mutual kindnesses that create a strong sense of security. Relationships within families break down when kindness is withheld.

Schools and workplaces that create and maintain a culture of kindness create pleasant experiences for all. When those in charge fail to instil a culture of kindness in their schools or workplaces, they inadvertently contribute to needless hurt and painful experiences for many.

THE ART OF KINSHIP

"Self-actualising people have a deep feeling of identification, sympathy and affection for human beings in general. They feel kinship and connection as if all people were members of a single family"

Maslow

Evolution underlines our innate kinship with all of life. When we disregard this sense of kinship we create division, prejudice and unfairness between people. We also disregard the welfare of other species and we inflict grievous harm on the planet we inhabit. Kinship with all life is the true essence of civilisation. There can be no greater purpose than the continuous betterment of all of life.

If we are ever going to finally end hunger and the needless suffering of millions of people we need to renounce greed and war for once and for all. If we are to end the incalculable suffering we cause to other species and fully respect the Earth itself, then we need to foster and expand a deep sense of innate kinship with all of life. We can do this in our schools, colleges, businesses and workplaces by emphasising our innate connection to all of life. We can strengthen our connection and commitment to live cooperatively with all of life by underpinning our political, economic and social policies with a fundamental sense of kinship with all of life.

Without these fundamental changes we are allowing the continuing destruction of the planet to go unchecked. The immense suffering of the many by the greed of the few continues on from one generation to the next. We could do so much better with a real sense and awareness of our innate kinship with all of life.

CHAPTER XII

THE POWER OF THE LAW OF ATTRACTION

"Know that this is a Universe that works on energy and attraction"

Wayne Dyer

Developing conscious awareness of the relationship between our thoughts and the universal energy force is key to understanding the power of the Law of Attraction.

Thoughts are energy that act as a magnet attracting like energy. In simple terms, when we are transmitting positive energy through our thinking we are attracting positive energy back to us. Conversely, when we are thinking negatively we are attracting negative energy back to ourselves.

We have an in-built emotional guidance system that lets us know when we need to change our thinking. Broadly speaking, we are either feeling good or feeling bad at any given moment. As energy only ever exists in the present we can change feeling bad to feeling good by changing the way we are thinking in the present moment. Feelings without specific thoughts to sustain them soon dissipate.

Thoughts that involve gratitude have high vibrational energy and can lift low energy feelings. Similarly, by using a positive affirmation repeatedly, such as the one used by the French psychologist, Émile Coue: "Every day in every way I am better and better", we can alter the energy that we attract to ourselves. Gratitude and affirmations are also very effective because they displace persistent negative thinking that can often be difficult to displace.

Achieving consistent change in the energy we draw to ourselves involves taking conscious control over our own thinking in each present moment. Our present thought vibration is the only one that matters as energy only exists in the now. We can use the power of the Law of Attraction to change our lives for the better at any time.

The Law of Attraction operates in our lives whether or not we are aware of it. For this reason it is important, when faced with any of life's problems, to shift our focus immediately away from the problem and to focus instead on potential solutions. When we continue to focus our mental energy on a problem we intensify the power and energy of that problem. If we shift the focus of our thoughts instead into solution mode we attract potential solutions to us.

Similarly, it is unwise to focus the energy of our thinking on the lack or absence of anything we desire. By focusing on lack we draw that same energy to us. It is infinitely more beneficial to focus on what we desire so that we draw the energy of abundance to us.

It is important to keep in mind what Lao Tzu was keen to emphasise. Namely, we attract the energy of what we are being at any given time. What we are being is what we are thinking, feeling or doing at any given time. For this reason it is in our own interest to let go of thoughts and feelings of anger and hatred. Being angry or feeling hatred or rage attracts similar energy back to ourselves.

Any negative thought process prevents us from connecting with a more powerful and more vibrant energy that is always available to us. By thinking higher energy thoughts of gratitude, love, joy or peace we can change our own energy field. How often we experience positive emotion is the best way to measure how successful we are at attracting good energy to ourselves.

THE ART OF LISTENING

"... most important , follow your heart and intuition, they somehow already know what you truly want to become"

Steve Jobs

Intuition is our innate guidance system that is always available to us throughout our lives. It is the guiding voice of our own higher intelligence. This explains the 'somehow' that Steve Jobs referred to when he said that our intuition somehow knows what we truly want to become.

When we listen to that guiding voice, we feel in our gut what is the right course of action to take. It's sole purpose is to inspire and guide us. If we want to know whether or not we are acting in accordance with our intuitive self we need only turn to our emotional guidance system. When we feel good we are acting in tune with our higher intelligence. When we are out of sync with that intelligence we feel down and out of sorts.

As our intuition can only ever communicate with us in the present moment we often fail to hear it. Our incessant thinking drowns out the inner voice. When we do succeed in hearing it, we often fail to trust it or we do not have the courage to follow it. This is because we doubt or we do not have a strong belief in the existence of our own higher intelligence or that of a higher consciousness.

When the same ideas call to us again and again and those ideas match our innate talents, then it is in our interest to pay close attention to those ideas. They let us know what we really want to do with our lives. These ideas usually persist for a time but drift away when we continue to ignore them. When we follow what is calling to us it gives us a sense of purpose and a feeling of fulfillment that enriches our lives. If we are truly fortunate, we may even succeed in making our living in this way. Or we may simply choose to pursue some project in our own time where the need to make money doesn't interfere with the creative process.

Either way we do not need fame or fortune to give us a sense of purpose or fulfillment. All that is required is the passionate pursuit of an inspired idea that may one day benefit the common good. It is likely to involve hours of committed endeavour where persistence is the key to overcoming obstacles. Finding pleasure in the process of pursuing a definite plan is success in itself.

We can enhance the art of listening to our own intuitive voice by beginning a regular practice of "sitting for ideas". When we sit in stillness we create the mental silence into which the light of our own higher intelligence can shine. It is our habit of incessant thinking that creates the mental clutter that drowns out the guiding voice of inspiration.

The ultimate purpose of all human existence is to contribute to the expansion of our own energy and the expansion of the universal energy system. When we doubt or do not believe in the existence of our own higher intelligence we fail to listen to it. So much human potential is lost because we do not listen to our own inspirational guidance system.

CHAPTER XIII

THE POWER OF MEDITATION

"It could be that meditation practice supplies something as absolutely essential as sleep or food or being loved"

Jan Chozen Bays

Our greatest tragedy is our tendency to focus all our energies on the human aspects of our lives, ignoring the immense power of our own higher intelligence which is our very essence.

In the *Tibetan Book of Living and Dying,* meditation is described as "the greatest gift you can give yourself in this life". This is because consciousness is at the core of who we are. Meditation which is outside the field of thought connects us to consciousness itself.

It is high time, as Wolf Singer pointed out, "to reconcile science with Western and Eastern intuitions". Singer believes that this is necessary if we are going to be able to cope with the practical and psychological challenges we are facing. Science as he rightly points out is just one of several sources of knowledge. It is not the all.

The World Health Organization has predicted that, if nothing is done to prevent it, depression will be the most common illness in 2030. Right now anxiety, stress, self-harm and suicide are at unacceptably high levels. Meditation has the power both to heal the heart and expand consciousness. Studies have shown that meditation improves physical, mental and emotional well-being. It lessens the habit of incessant thinking which then allows us to live more in the present moment. We gain a new kind of clarity in our thinking processes and a new sense of emotional equilibrium. We become far more organized and productive on the days when we take time out to meditate than on the days when we are too busy to do so.

Meditation is the primary route to reaching our full individual and collective potential. It opens the door to that dimension which, when aligned with it, allows us to move forward with tremendous power.

There are many different kinds of meditation practice. In his excellent book, *Silence Your Mind*, Dr. Ramesh Manocha stresses "the central importance of mental silence in meditation". Mental silence is the space between each thought. With practice that space expands. Although he has not recommended it I have found that repeating the words "mental silence" like a mantra is one way of achieving that state.

And if, as Gandhi suggested, "the soul can see its path clearly through silence", then that alone is reason enough to embark on the practice of meditation or mental silence.

THE ART OF MEANING

"Ask what makes you come alive and go and do that"

Walt Whitman

Creating meaning in our lives fills what Viktor Frankl referred to as "the existential vacuum that is the mass neuroses of the present time". When we have a sense of meaning and a sense of purpose we experience far greater life satisfaction.

As the human manifestation of universal energy we have the power to create good and the power to create harm. There is no neutral. Peace, as Mother Teresa said, begins with a smile. Everything we think, feel, say and do contributes to the expansion of either beneficial or harmful energy. A small minority can actively create great harm across the world, especially when the majority stay silent in relation to inequality and injustice.

Depending on our own unique talents and values, we can all make our lives count for something. It may be something we work at or something we pursue in our free time that contributes to the common good. Over a lifetime the meaning and purpose that we create is likely to change many times depending on our changing circumstances and values.

We would all benefit from a keen awareness of what constitutes the common good. By stepping away from a self-centered lifestyle, filled with insatiable wants, we could refocus, in part at least, on benefiting those we encounter. Every day presents us with opportunities to contribute to the pleasure or pain of the lives of others.

The pull and push between the forces of good and harm is played out daily on this planet. Every moment we exist, by our thoughts, feelings and actions, we are contributing consciously or unconsciously to either the good or the harmful energy in the universe. There is no neutral. By our self-centered lifestyles and tolerance of widespread injustices we unwittingly aid the side that is intent on harm and destruction.

We can live a life that has meaning and purpose by extending kindnesses to one another and becoming actively engaged in the pursuit of anything that benefits the common good. In this way we benefit the universal energy system.

CHAPTER XIV

THE POWER OF NEGATIVITY

"Whining is the least appropriate response to suffering"

Leonard Cohen

The power of negativity to adversely affect our lives cannot be overstated. It is essential to challenge our negative attitudes and negative thinking processes if we want to improve our mental and emotional well-being.

Negativity results in an underlying sense of dissatisfaction with life in general and with one's own life in particular. It causes needless stress and anxiety, low mood, and feelings of resentment.

The tendency to blame events, circumstances or other people for our feelings or our actions does not serve us well. It weakens rather than strengthens our character. It is only by accepting full responsibility for how we think, feel and act that we take command of our own lives. Similarly, constant complaining does nothing to help us. It keeps the focus of our attention on what we feel is lacking in our lives rather than appreciating what we already have. Always wanting things to be other than they are, makes for a dissatisfied life.

One of the most damaging thought processes that we routinely adopt is worrying about outcomes. Far too often it is our primary response to difficulties as they arise. Worrying has no beneficial effect on outcomes. It creates so much needless stress and anxiety. Stress is a key component in physical, mental and emotional ill-health.

We cannot always control outcomes. What we can do is explore the pros and cons of the actions we can take. Good judgement and decision-making processes rely on the clarity of our thinking which is diminished when we spend our time worrying. Dealing effectively with challenging situations requires positively focused mental processes. For our own peace of mind we must always be willing to accept the things we cannot change.

To develop strength of character and resilience it is essential to refrain from blaming, complaining or worrying. Rather than crumbling under the weight of our challenges, we can rise to meet each one. We strengthen our own inner resources by drawing repeatedly on them and we do much better when we expect more of ourselves.

On the occasions when feelings of pain, hurt, loss and grief are unavoidable it is vitally important to acknowledge and explore those feelings rather than suppress them. There is nothing negative about sadness as a response to the loss of health, work or loved ones.

Suffering in this way is difficult but in all circumstances it is better to avoid the trap that is self-pity. Self-pity leads to perceiving ourselves as a victim which can lead to a feeling of powerlessness. Healing happens naturally through grieving our loss, self-nurture, support from others and the passage of time.

THE ART OF NURTURE

"Take care of the body, it's the only place you have to live"

Jim Rohn

Ill-health can be one of life's most difficult challenges. Yet we often take good health for granted. That is, until it comes under serious threat. While we cannot control all aspects of our health we can do things that nurture our physical, mental and emotional well-being. Here are 10 examples of how we can nurture our physical, mental and emotional well-being.

1. Be aware how the foods you regularly consume affect your overall health. Avoid consuming calories at a greater rate than you burn them.
2. Maintain a healthy balance between the time spent on the move and the time you spend sitting down.
3. Keep the body properly hydrated by drinking water throughout the day. This helps to combat fatigue.
4. As often as possible get sufficient and restful sleep. Early

nights make for a better sleep experience. Successive late nights can make the day ahead seem like an uphill struggle.

5. Maintain a positive disposition as far as possible. Negative thoughts create and sustain low mood.
6. When experiencing stress, always deal with the root cause of it. Prolonged stress can damage your health.
7. Relaxation is the natural antidote to stress and also helps to build resilience against stressful situations.
8. Let go of anger and resentment. They are extremely harmful to your physical, mental and emotional well-being.
9. Rather than ruminating endlessly on a problem, focus instead on potential solutions.
10. Find joy each day by indulging in some of life's many pleasures.

CHAPTER XV

THE POWER OF ORDINARY PEOPLE

"The earth is a generous mother. She will provide in plentiful abundance, food for all her children, if they will but cultivate her soil in justice and in peace"

William Cockran

The best chance we will ever have of a peaceful and just world is for ordinary people to use their collective power to demand it. We are one species and our differences in gender, colour, race, sexuality or creed are but a convenient and effective way of ensuring that ordinary workers do not become united. It suits the wealthy powerful elite when ordinary working people rail against each other on grounds of race for example. Income inequality is one crucial difference between us all.

As long as ordinary people defer to authority and blindly accept the spin that the corporate owned and mainstream media constantly peddle, a shameful income inequality will continue to be the norm. Deference is as dangerous as fear, according to the author, Philip Petit. Ordinary people need to be brave enough to speak out. By actively lobbying and by peaceful protest we can make our collective voices heard.

We need a new kind of Nations for Peace entity with millions of members across the globe lobbying and marching for peace and justice. The indecent haste and lack of due care of the post colonial redrawing of borders needs to be revisited and amicably revised where everyone must compromise something for the greater good of all.

While democracy as we know it is far from perfect, it is preferable to authoritarian rule of any kind that facilitates corruption and the gross misuse of power. It is up to each generation to determine its own legacy. Tolerating endless wars and gross injustice diminishes all of us and reflects shamefully on our species.

THE ART OF OTHER PEOPLE

"Unthinking respect for authority is the greatest enemy of truth"

Albert Einstein

Being true to ourselves is the essence of living an authentic life. As long as we do no harm we have the right not to allow the good or bad opinion of others to inhibit or dictate our actions.

Equally important is the adoption of a non-judgemental attitude to other people. As long as others are doing no harm they are free to focus on their own actions and aspirations. Sitting in judgement on other people is time and energy wasted. It also accounts for the accumulation of so much needless mental clutter.

According to Einstein, the most important question facing humanity and the first and most basic question that all people must answer for themselves is whether you live in a friendly or hostile universe. How we answer this question has profound political and personal implications as it determines our view of other people and of the universe itself. When we decide that the universe is an unfriendly place then according to Einstein we use our technology and our scientific resources to achieve safety and power by creating bigger walls and bigger weapons to keep out the unfriendliness. The real battle then is to convince hearts and minds that this is indeed a friendly universe where science and technology can be used to create stability and safety rather than furthering division and hostility. Fostering and nurturing the fundamental belief that other people are not the enemy is of paramount importance.

Part Four

CHAPTER XVI

THE POWER OF PERSISTENCE

"There is one elementary truth the ignorance of which kills countless ideas and splendid plans ... the moment we commit then Providence moves too"

Goethe

Goethe went on to say that all sorts of things occur to help one that would not otherwise have occurred once we commit ourselves to any aspiration. Carl Jung referred to these acts of Providence as synchronicity or meaningful coincidences.

Ideas and plans, if they are to be realised, require our full commitment. It can be difficult to maintain one's commitment over a long period of time. The inevitability of meeting obstacles along the way can severely test one's commitment. The temptation then to abandon a plan or idea may be overwhelming. To sustain commitment persistence is key.

Giving up is all too easy and far too common. Half-hearted efforts are rarely rewarded. With persistence the seemingly impossible becomes possible as invisible forces find a way through. Once we are prepared to persist in our commitment, solutions invariably present themselves to us.

Our potential to realise ideas and plans that benefit ourselves and our world is enormous. When our commitment begins to falter it is time to ride the wild horses of commitment and persistence and drive on in whatever direction destiny is beckoning.

THE ART OF PERSPECTIVE

"Pessimism is a waste of time"

Norman Cousins

There is no doubt that perspective plays a significant role in physical, mental and emotional well-being. Our thought patterns affect the cells in our bodies. Not surprisingly, an optimistic perspective has a significantly beneficial effect on the body's chemistry while a persistently negative outlook is harmful to our overall health.

One of the symptoms of a negative perspective is the tendency to constantly worry about one thing or another. Worrying is a fear-based response to change and uncertainty. While the futility of worrying may be self-evident, its harmful effects are less so. Worry induces stress which adversely affects the body's chemistry and negatively impacts our mental and emotional well-being.

Change and uncertainty are integral to the nature of existence. We cannot control everything that happens to us. Nor will everything always turn out the way we would have wished. Accepting change and making peace with uncertainty frees us from a fear-based perspective. No longer resisting the flow of life we cease to waste time and energy pulling and pushing against the Universe.

Perspective is also adversely affected when we engage in blaming, complaining, feeling guilty or holding on to grudges and regrets. By clearing out this kind of mental clutter we are free to live from the simple perspective of appreciating being alive all the while maintaining as optimistic an outlook as possible.

There will be occasions when significant loss or serious illness will affect us directly or indirectly. At times like these it is perfectly natural to experience feelings of anguish, sadness, even despair. These are normal responses to traumatic events. It is important not to suppress these feelings but to grieve and work through them. Challenges build character and compassion and very often it is our biggest challenges that lead us in new and rewarding directions.

CHAPTER XVII

THE POWER OF QUIET

"Quiet people have the loudest minds"

Stephen Hawking

In the field of psychology it is generally accepted that where we come on the introvert/extrovert spectrum forms the basis of our personality. Even though introversion is more valued in the East than in the West, research indicates that between one third and half the population is predominantly introverted. Yet the pressure on introverts to present themselves as extroverts, in order to fit in, is immense.

Susan Cain, in her book *Quiet*, explores the power of introversion. She explains how the current culture has created an oppressive standard to which most introverts feel they must conform. The effort involved in subverting the most fundamental dimension of one's personality often causes what Cain refers to as deep psychic pain.

Knowing yourself and being true to that self is the essence of being comfortable in your own skin and comfortable in the world around you. For those of us who are predominantly introverted, too much social stimulation depletes one's energy. Too much time spent alone depletes the energy of the predominantly extroverted. To recharge, introverts need to spend time alone while extroverts recharge their energy in the company of others. This awareness is fundamental to both types of personality if we are to thrive rather than flounder.

Like any spectrum, extreme introversion and extreme extroversion are not desirable. Most people have elements of both but are predominantly one or the other. It makes sense for us to value what both kinds of personality have to offer. As Carl Jung pointed out, introverts are drawn to the world of thought and feeling while extroverts are drawn to the external life of people and activities.

Our current culture, particularly in the West, needs to acknowledge the value of both. We need to end the subtle oppression of the predominantly introverted.

Introverts need to assert their right to be true to themselves. Susan Cain recommends remaining squarely inside our comfort zone when it comes to our interaction with others. She also recommends giving up being apologetic, defensive or trying to meet the expectations of others.

THE ART OF QUOTATION

"The whole of life, from the moment you are born to the moment you die, is a process of learning"

Krishnamurti

Not all quotations are full of wisdom but very many right down through the ages have much to teach us. Wise quotations are one of the most efficient and effective ways of learning about life. So much wisdom in so few words.

CHAPTER XVIII

THE POWER OF RELATIONSHIPS

"Nothing can make our life or the lives of others more beautiful than perpetual kindness"

Leo Tolstoy

There can be no doubt that relationships significantly impact the quality of all our lives. For this reason it is worth investing time and effort cultivating good authentic relationships. To do this we need to be our authentic self. Our primary relationship is with ourselves. For that relationship to be truly healthy it needs to be based on self-acceptance. Once we accept ourselves unconditionally, we can then nurture ourselves by practicing unconditional self-love. By being our own best friend we honour and take care of ourselves first and foremost.

To live authentically it is essential to know oneself and to be oneself. It is important to recognise one's strengths, weaknesses and one's innate talents. There is little value in living an inauthentic life. To be true to ourselves we must demonstrate the courage to be ourselves regardless of the circumstances. It is vital that we free ourselves from the gaze and the good or bad opinion of others. This can inhibit us and prevent us from being our authentic selves. There is no honour in being false. Nor is there much honour in being a people pleaser.

We relate to ourselves and others through our thoughts, feelings and above all through our actions. By cultivating hearts and minds that operate out of kindness we become more generous in our actions towards ourselves and others. When we have a dysfunctional relationship with ourselves through self-recrimination, or with others by harbouring resentment, we cause ourselves and others much needless angst and hurt. There is endless joy and pleasure to be had when we extend loving kindness to ourselves and to others. Good relationships improve our quality of life in so many ways. The time and effort that we invest in cultivating authentic and long lasting relationships will be of enormous benefit to us throughout our lives.

THE ART OF RELAXATION

"If you want to conquer the anxiety of life,
live in the moment, live in the breath"

Amit Ray

There is no doubt that stress undermines our health and our well-being. Prolonged stress undermines our immune system, leaving us susceptible to illness. Aside from potential illness, a stressful lifestyle depletes our energy and vitality for life. Common causes of stress are financial or relationship difficulties and lack of advance planning or work overload.

The natural antidote to stress is relaxation. Relaxation not only reduces our stress levels but even more importantly, when practiced regularly, it minimizes the accumulation of more stress. A key way to combat stress is to consciously incorporate as many forms of relaxation as possible into one's everyday lifestyle.

One of the easiest and most effective ways of incorporating relaxation into our daily lives is the practice of deep breathing.

One very effective method is to breathe in to the count of 4, hold to the count of 4 and then breathe out to the count of 8. By doing this consistently any number of times each day, especially on waking up and when going to sleep, we can begin and end each day in a more relaxed state. The more time we spend practicing deep breathing the more relaxed we become. Deep breathing is also a way of ridding the body of harmful toxins. It even has some of the same benefits as aerobic exercise. Regularly practicing deep breathing is also a very effective way of overcoming shyness.

Possibly the most effective tool in the art of relaxation is the practice of mental silence. Like anything else, the practice of mental silence is a skill that can be learned and improved with practice. The myriad benefits of sitting in stillness and silencing the mind are well documented. When practiced consistently mental silence allows us to live more in the present moment. It is scientifically proven to benefit our physical, mental and emotional well-being and it enables us to access our innate creativity far more easily.

Fatigue is a common side-effect of a stressful lifestyle. The easiest and quickest way to combat fatigue is to ensure sufficient and restful sleep. It is important to drink lots of water throughout the day so that the body remains properly hydrated. Including some form of aerobic exercise in our normal routine also helps to reduce stress and increases energy levels.

Tension held in the neck and back muscles can be relieved by deep tissue or ki massage. Hippocrates, the acknowledged father of western medicine, regarded massage and aromatherapy as key treatments in the maintenance of good health. Burning essential oils like chamomile or rose in the home or workplace allows us to breathe in deeply sensual and relaxing aromas as we go about our day. To combat trouble sleeping a few drops of lavender on the pillow should help and early nights help to effectively combat fatigue.

Being disorganised causes much needless stress and so much wasted time. By decluttering our physical environment and by using lists to plan both our work and personal time, we not only achieve far more but feel more relaxed doing so. Adopting a non-judgemental attitude to other people is also a wonderful way to further reduce needless mental clutter.

If we want to live a more relaxed lifestyle, we can do so by breaking the habit of worrying about what other people might think or about events that may or may not happen. We cannot control everything all of the time. We can do what we can to improve any situation but we need to be able to accept that uncertainty is an integral part of life. Worry is the root cause of so much stress and it achieves nothing. Looking back at the end of our lives, not only will we wish that we had worried less but it is far more likely that we will wish we had not worried at all.

CHAPTER XIX

THE POWER OF SOURCE ENERGY

"An intelligence system greater than the human mind is at work"

Eckhart Tolle

Everything that exists is part of one universal energy system. Manifested in human form we are part of the greater intelligence system from which everything emanates.

This greater intelligence system only ever exists in the eternal present moment. It is by maintaining awareness in the present that we are inspired and guided.

When we are consciously seeing, consciously hearing, consciously tasting, consciously smelling and consciously touching we are aligned with the greater intelligence system.

Far too often we become lost in thought, operating on autopilot. By failing to consciously see, hear, taste, smell or touch what is in our immediate experience we lose the immense power of inspiration and guidance that is available to us in each present moment.

While we are highly evolved beings, we are not the All. Living as if human intelligence is the highest intelligence system in the universe often causes us to experience an underlying sense of anxiety, dissatisfaction and lack of meaning or purpose. More importantly, the loss of potential for us, both individually and collectively, is incalculable.

It is only by engaging the power of the higher intelligence in the art of being that we live life as it was originally intended.

THE ART OF STILLNESS

"There is a benevolent force flowing through all reality. When you are aligned with that force you move forward with tremendous power"

Lao Tzu

The universe is evolving all the time and we are part of that evolution. Consciousness is the universal intelligence or energy system from which everything emanates. This intelligence system is far greater than human intelligence.

Eckhart Tolle believes that we can save and transform our world by taking the next step in human evolution. We do this by transcending thought. To transcend thought we need to be in alignment with the power of stillness.

By focusing on the breath and by sensing the animating presence, within and without, we align with stillness. By shifting the focus of our attention away from the world around us and onto our innermost self we sit in the awareness of the greater consciousness.

We maintain this awareness through mental silence, all the time aware of the flow of energy. When thoughts intrude we simply need to gently shift our attention back to the breath and the flow of energy, within and without.

Listening to stillness, in alignment with the higher intelligence force, we can access our innate guidance system. It is from this source that inspiration and creativity flow. When we return our focus to the world around us we can maintain our connection to inspiration and guidance by being present in our own experience. Lost in thought we are not present in the now moment. By our conscious presence in our own energy field and the energy field around us we honour life.

Intuitive guidance is there to guide us. It whispers to us through this channel of communication that exists between our minds and consciousness itself. When in alignment, serendipity and synchronicity play a far greater role in our lives. This is what Carl Jung referred to as "meaningful coincidences".

Each of us is responsible for how we evolve. When we allow the power of consciousness to work through us we discover our true purpose. This involves using our innate talents for the common good and ultimately for the benefit of the evolution of the universe itself. It is this that gives life it's true meaning and purpose.

CHAPTER XX

THE POWER OF THOUGHT

"The thoughts we choose to think are the tools we use to paint the canvas of our lives"

Louise Hay

It is infinitely better to spend less time in thought and more time living in the awareness of our immediate sensory experience. Nonetheless it is vitally important to understand the immense power that our thoughts exert over our lives.

Thoughts are energy that act like a magnet. They attract back energy to us that is of a similar vibration. If we want to attract energy that is beneficial rather than harmful it is imperative that we pay close attention to the kinds of thoughts we are habitually thinking. For this reason we would do well to heed the words of

Wayne Dyer when he suggested that we allow only prosperous thoughts to live in our consciousness.

Every day is a fresh opportunity to take creative control over our own thinking process. By doing this we maintain creative control over our own lives. Often our thoughts encompass both our hopes and our fears. Focused on our hopes we draw energy around us that helps us to advance in the direction of our dreams. When we focus instead on our fears we draw energy to us that renders us anxious and causes us to feel stressed and powerless.

Our thoughts and our feelings are inextricably linked. Our feelings reflect the kind of thoughts we are thinking. For example, when we are thinking thoughts that involve anger, blame, hate, intolerance, resentment or self-pity, we tend to feel upset and dissatisfied. These feelings are self-inflicted and will only change when we change our thinking. We can, if we choose, work gradually to eradicate this kind of harmful thinking from our own thought processes.

In their place, we can start each day with an open frame of mind, a mind filled with curiosity and wonder for what lies ahead. When we accept uncertainty as an intrinsic part of the nature of existence, we are then able to let go of worry. Worrying about outcomes has no beneficial effect on how things turn out. It adversely affects our physical, mental and emotional well- being. Put simply, stressful and anxious thoughts cause us to feel stressed and anxious.

Similarly, when we are non-judgemental in our thinking, we free our minds from so much needless clutter. Likewise when we decide to be someone who is easily pleased rather than someone who is easily irritated, we cease to habitually think many of the thoughts that adversely affect our mood.

We also discover then that there is a lot less to think about. This in turn makes it easier to live more in the awareness of our immediate sensory experience and to use our thinking processes for the short, medium and long-term planning of our aspirations and obligations.

THE ART OF TIME

"Well arranged time is the surest mark of a well-arranged life"

Isaac Pitman

Time is a human construct that when skilfully arranged gives us much greater control over our lives. Arranging time well is a simple skill that can make an enormous difference to our lives. How we value this limited resource reflects how we value life itself.

To arrange time effectively we need to be cognisant of both our aspirations and our obligations. A well-arranged life will incorporate both comfortably. Advance planning is the key to well-arranged time. Plans that are written down with specific time frames focus the mind on the "what" and the "when" of how our aspirations will be attempted and how our obligations may be met.

Daily to-do lists with detailed specific time pockets keep our minds focused on the task at hand by creating units of attention for each one. We get more done in less time when we formulate units of attention for what we need or want to achieve.

Unfulfilled aspirations and unmet obligations are very often the result of procrastination. By including both our aspirations and our obligations on a daily to-do list, we can begin to shift the burden of guilt and regret that so often accompanies aspirations that have not been as yet attempted and obligations that we have yet to fulfil.

The importance of ensuring sufficient time for sleep cannot be overstated. We achieve far less when we are tired. We are also more easily irritated which affects all our relationships. Early nights provide the restorative qualities necessary for our overall well being.

And of course, a well-arranged life will always seek to create time pockets for the sole purpose of experiencing the joy of simple pleasures and the nurturing feeling that is relaxation.

PART FIVE

CHAPTER XXI

THE POWER OF UNCONDITIONAL LOVE

"I believe that unarmed truth and unconditional love will have the final word."

Martin Luther King Jr

Unconditional love is the highest form of energy vibration that we can generate. Somewhere between the extremes of unconditional love and unadulterated hatred is the energy we create and generate by the kindnesses and unkindnesses that we engage in on a daily basis.

Operating from unconditional love on a consistent basis is not easily achieved. Nonetheless, it is possible to find a pathway through kindness that will at least take us in the right direction along the spectrum from low to high vibrational energy.

When we free our hearts from greed and hatred , we create a higher vibrational energy. By simply operating out of kindness we could transform life as we know it. That we do not do so is our greatest tragedy. We all know life for everyone could be so much better. How hard can it be to swap greed for generosity and unkindness for kindness.

THE ART OF UNDERSTANDING

"There is a moment when we have to transcend the side we are on and realise we are creatures of a higher order"

Leonard Cohen

Understanding our true nature and our purpose here is fundamental to realizing our full potential. If we accept that it is reasonable to assume the existence of an intelligence system greater than our human intelligence then it is reasonable to conclude that we are indeed creatures of a higher order.

To transcend the side we are on, we have to look beyond the human constructs that are nation states and religious belief systems. We are an evolving species which creates and generates both beneficial and harmful energy. As energy channels, this world is our opportunity to actively minimize or inhibit as far as possible the creation and generation of harmful energy.

We are each responsible for the kind of energy we generate. For this reason it is important to maintain an awareness of the energy we are creating through our thoughts, feelings and actions. This not only affects our own evolution but it affects the evolution of the entire universal energy system. It is our choice whether we are contributing beneficial or harmful energy in any given moment throughout our lives.

CHAPTER XXII

THE POWER OF VIBRATION

"The ether is a great cosmic mass of
eternal forces of vibration"

Theo Gimble

Einstein said that everything in life is vibration. As energy manifested in human form we too contribute to the great cosmic mass of vibrations. Our contribution can be beneficial or it can be harmful. This is why what we are thinking, feeling or doing matters greatly as that is the energy we are creating and generating at any given time.

To ensure that we contribute beneficial rather than harmful vibrations to the great cosmic mass our thoughts, feelings and actions need to revolve around generosity and kindness rather than greed and unkindness. This is how we can contribute to making the world a better place for all.

We can minimize our contribution to harmful energy vibrations by minimizing the kind of thoughts, feelings and actions that are generated by anger and resentment of one kind or another.

As we are each free to choose our own thoughts, which are intrinsically linked to our feelings and ultimately our actions, we are each responsible for the kind of vibrations we transmit. As like attracts like we are also responsible for many of the good or hostile vibrations we attract back to ourselves.

To make a difference, not just in our own lives but in the lives of others, we can begin to consciously transmit good vibrations as often as possible and to consciously minimize our transmission of harmful vibrations. In this way each of us can make an enormous difference to the great cosmic mass of vibrations.

THE ART OF VISUALISATION

"Imagination is the beginning of creation. You imagine what you desire, you will what you imagine, and at last, you create what you will."

George Bernard Shaw

Visualisation is the art of using one's imagination to attract specific energy to create what we want in our lives. By believing with absolute certainty in the potential realisation of what we repeatedly imagine we attract the necessary energy for its realisation.

We can use visualisation to create specific energy in any area of our lives. This might involve repeatedly imagining ourselves enjoying better health, finances, relationships or work situations. Once we picture a specific image repeatedly in our mind's eye we are creating that energy. We attract that energy to us by continuing to believe with absolute certainty in its potential realisation.

It is extremely important not to dwell on any doubts we may have in relation to the process itself or the desired outcome.

Doubts interrupt the process of attracting specific energy. Persistent doubts undermine the entire process by blocking the flow of the energy created through visualisation.

Visualisation can also be used as a powerful tool in helping us to achieve a long-held aspiration. This works best when our specific aspiration matches our innate talents. By repeatedly creating a picture in our mind's eye, of what achieving our aspiration looks like, we create the specific energy that helps us to move forward in the direction of our goal.

This energy appears in our lives in different shapes and guises as long as we continue to believe with absolute certainty in the potential realisation of an aspiration. It may be a flash of inspiration, a great idea that simply pops into our minds. It may be something that someone says to us. Or it may be something that we see, hear or read. What is important is that we remain alert so that we recognise the signs of opportunity as they present themselves to us. These are what Carl Jung referred to as meaningful coincidences.

It is useful to remember that we are at all times creating and attracting energy. Rather than doing this by default, we have the capacity to create and attract better energy by controlling and improving our thought processes, our belief systems and in turn our imaginative capabilities.

CHAPTER XXIII

THE POWER OF WORDS

"If you believe in the power of words you can bring about physical changes in the universe"

H. Scott Momaday

By believing in the power of words we each have the ability to create change. As human beings we create and generate energy at all times. When we are not consciously doing so we create and generate energy by default.

According to Lao Tzu the kind of energy we create and generate reflects what we are being at any given moment. What we are being is intrinsically linked to our thought process. We think in words. As words are central to the thought process, they exert an enormous influence over the kind of energy we create and generate in our lives.

For this reason it is essential to heed the advice of Wayne Dyer: 'allow only prosperous thoughts to live in your consciousness'. To create and attract the energy of prosperity we need to consistently use words that denote prosperity rather than lack in our lives. What we are being is reflected in the feel good factor that arises from thinking prosperous thoughts. We then attract and generate the kind of high vibrational energy that is in alignment with what we are being.

It is important to be aware that the opposite is also true. When we consistently think in words that focus on problems or on what is lacking in any area of our lives, we create low mood feelings within ourselves. We then attract and generate a low energy vibration that is in alignment with what we are being in that moment.

Fortunately for us, it is we ourselves who control the words we use when we are engaged in thinking. By choosing our words with greater care we can better control our mood and the kind of vibrational energy we create and generate in each present moment. This is one way we can each use the power of words more effectively throughout our lives.

THE ART OF WORK

"Opportunities are usually disguised as hard work so most people don't recognise them."

Ann Landers

The value of working hard in any area of life cannot be overstated. Far too often it is lack of effort rather than inability that prevents us from realizing our full potential. Hard work presents us with opportunities that bring many and varied rewards.

Teaching children the value of a good work ethic bestows on them a lifelong gift. While working hard to get an education might not get them their dream job, it can go a long way towards lifting generations out of poverty. Often, against the odds, an inspiring parent, guardian or teacher can instil not just a love of learning but also a knowledge of the practical rewards that hard work brings.

When it comes to our home environment, there are significant rewards for working hard to maintain a clean and tidy living space. A cluttered home adversely affects the equilibrium of those who live in it. Putting in the effort to maintain order in our private sanctuaries creates an atmosphere that better supports our mood and hence our relationships.

Working hard also reflects how we value our time. Without commitment, effort and persistence so much talent lies dormant because of a lack of effort on our part.

However limited our free time may be, it is possible to make time, however short, to nurture our innate creativity. Whether through art or craft, we can satisfy the hunger to be creative that is an innate part of what it is to be a human being.

In his memoir, *Hillbilly Elegy*, J.D. Vance says that what he would most like to change is the feeling that our choices don't matter. There is, he says, something powerful about realising that you've undersold yourself and that somehow your mind confused lack of effort with inability.

CHAPTER XXIV

THE POWER OF "X"

"Remembering that I'll soon be dead is the most important tool I've ever encountered to help me make the big choices in life"

Steve Jobs

The beauty and power of X is that it can be whatever you want it to be. X is that which, on your deathbed, you will be glad you chose to do it.

THE ART OF "X"

"... most important, have the courage to follow your heart and intuition; they somehow already know what you truly want to become"

Steve Jobs

To quote Rumi, "What you seek is seeking you". By listening in stillness we can better hear the ideas that call to us again and again. When these ideas match our innate talents, we would do well to pursue them with commitment, effort and persistence. The art of X is to do that which allows us to have few, if any, regrets and to know that we have lived a life we can be proud of.

CHAPTER XXV

THE POWER OF YOU

"There is a universal, intelligent life force that exists within everyone and everything"

Shakti Gawain

As energy that has manifested in human form we are part of the universal intelligence system. This intelligence force is far greater than our human intelligence. As an integral part of this system we are always connected to it.

This intelligence system only ever exists in the eternal present moment. Its guidance is therefore only available to us when we are aware in our moment by moment present experience. Then, and only then, are we at one with our innate guidance system through which ideas and inspiration flow.

Awareness in our present moment experience opens our connection to our intuitive guidance. Paying attention to our gut feelings and listening to our inner voice offers valuable guidance to us throughout our lives. The practice of mental silence and stillness leads to heightened awareness. It is how we come to better know ourselves and our place in the world.

THE ART OF YOU

"I am the master of my fate/I am the captain of my soul"

W. E. Henley (*Invictus*)

Socrates believed the unexamined life was not worth living. In more recent times Thoreau decided to "live deliberately" so that when he came to die he would not discover that he had not lived. Self-mastery involves examining one's life and living deliberately. Deciding what is important to us and deliberately choosing to do what reflects our values gives us better creative control over our lives. As we are each the artist in residence in our own lives we are each the creative director of our life. We are therefore responsible for the choices that we make everyday.

There are many ways to create a meaningful and purposeful life. Here are ten of the most important ways:

1. Self-care through unconditional self-acceptance and self-love. Whether you are an extrovert or an introvert, be true

to your authentic self. Be your own best friend and look after your physical, mental and emotional well being.

2. Make peace with your past. Holding on to resentment is, to quote Augustine, "drinking poison and waiting for the other person to die".

3. Live in the awareness of your present moment experience by spending less time thinking. In the words of Ram Dass, 'Be Here Now'.

4. When you engage in thinking, heed the words of Wayne Dyer and "allow only prosperous thoughts to live in your consciousness".

5. When you are feeling down remember Krisnamurti said 'if thought doesn't give continuity to feeling, feeling dies very quickly'.

6. Be assertive. Open, honest and direct communication makes for better relationships. Be non-judgemental in relation to others and it will free your mind from unnecessary clutter. And remember that being kind has a built-in feel good factor.

7. Harness your own will power. Determination and persistence are key to achieving the things that give our lives meaning and purpose.

8. Always try to live within your means. Bear in mind Mr. Macamber's advice to the young David Copperfield, "An-

nual income twenty pounds, annual expenditure nineteen, nineteen six. Result happiness. Annual income twenty pounds, annual expenditure twenty pounds nought and six, result misery".

9. Indulge in life's many pleasures as much as possible. Pleasure is an antidote to life's inevitable struggles and strife. Do more of what you enjoy doing and less of the things that you do not enjoy.

10. Develop the practice of stilling the mind. Mental silence leads to clarity of thought. You will come to know yourself better and will have greater access to your intuition which is your innate guidance system.

Part Six

CHAPTER XXVI

THE POWER OF THE ZEITGEIST

"What is needed is a shift in the political zeitgeist as many are realizing that the future depends on our ability to come together"

Naomi Klein

Across the world our political systems have allowed a tiny minority to amass the vast majority of all global assets. Unless we come together to create a radical shift in the political zeitgeist the gap in income levels will continue to widen.

Inequality has long been at the heart of virtually all our political and economic systems. This has resulted in obscene levels of private wealth alongside equally obscene levels of poverty. To change this, ordinary people have to come together and become actively engaged at a local, national and international level. Creating a worldwide movement for income fairness and environmental protection is possible but it depends on our ability to come together to create a shift in the political zeitgeist.

Our democracies have been undermined by the tech industry and by the enormous influence that business interests and corporate power are allowed to have over government policies.

Just because, in some countries at least, we get to vote every few years does not mean we live in thriving democracies. As Mark Twain pointed out "if voting made any difference they wouldn't let us do it".

For too long we have allowed ourselves to become divided and distracted by issues of gender, ethnicity, race, religion and sexuality. This principle of divide and conquer has always worked in favour of the wealthy elite. This pattern will continue if we allow ourselves to be distracted by these spurious concocted divisions. The only significant difference between any of us is our income level and the good or harm that we do here during our lifetime.

Our action or inaction now will be the legacy we leave behind for future generations. We will not be here forever and some things are worth fighting for. Unless we organise and begin to march for income fairness and environmental protection the gap between the obscenely rich and the obscenely poor will continue to widen and our planet will be damaged beyond repair. That will be our legacy to future generations. The real tragedy is the silence of the many, which if it continues, may well prove to be catastrophic for all of us. What is required is beautifully rendered by Russell Banks in the closing pages of his wonderful novel, Continental Drift :

"We are the planet, fully as much as its water, earth, fire and air are the planet, and if the planet survives, it will only be through heroism. Not occasional heroism, a remarkable instance of it here and there, but constant heroism, systematic heroism, heroism as governing principles."

THE ART OF ZEST

"Give me the comma of imperfect striving, thus to find zest in the immediate living"

Winston Graham

Zest is both an attitude and a feeling that gives us a wonderful sense of empowerment. It is a love of life. Without it life can seem routine and mundane. When we let go of that sense of zest for life we can end up taking life itself for granted.

Having something to strive for helps to maintain a keen sense of zest. Once we are committed and actively engaged in the pursuit of any aspiration, great or small, that pursuit becomes its own reward. Sooner or later our time here will end. It is by living with a sense of zest that we honour life and contribute a higher form of energy to the universal energy system. The kind of energy that we create and generate during our lifetime to that energy system is the legacy we leave behind when we die. This is our one true purpose on this planet.